Peace/ La Paix

Ballades et contes en quête de vérité

Hugh Fox

HHB

Higganum Hill Books : Higganum, Connecticut

First Edition
First Printing September 1, 2008

Higganum Hill Books
P.O. Box 666, Higganum, CT 06441
Phone (860) 345-4103
Email: rcdebold@mindspring.com

Library of Congress Control Number: 2008004625
ISBN13: 978-1-60585-181-5

Cover Image: Albrecht Dürer, *Knight, Death and the Devil (1513)*
Frontispiece: William Blake, 1757-1827.

Library of Congress Cataloging-in-Publication Data

Fox, Hugh, 1932-
   Peace = La paix : ballades et contes en quête de vérité / Hugh
Fox. -- 1st ed.
      p. cm.
   Poems in English, some with additional French or Portuguese
translations.
   ISBN 978-1-60585-181-5 (alk. paper)
   I. Title. II. Title: Paix.
   PS3556.O9P43 2008
   811'.54--dc22
                                        2008004625

Independent Publishers Group distributes Higganum Hill Books.
Phone: (800) 888-4741   www.ipgbook.com
Printed in the United States of America.

Dedication

TO GRANDMA MARY ROOS (MANGAN)
THE ONLY DOOR I COULD KNOCK ON
AND HAVE IT OPENED WITH LOVE AND
NOT SERMONIZING.

CONTENTS

Mercy and Truth are met together:
righteousness and peace have kissed each other.
– *Old Testament, Psalm lxxxv. 10.*

La PAIX – Museum Mark Aurele Fortin

La paix, la paix,
la paix, je suis
Muselman-juif,
Chretienne-Athée
come vous voulez, mais
quel importe, les arbres,
le ciel, un peu cle Satie dans
l'air, les saisons changent,
les jambs, les seins, les visages,
toute reviennt archaeologiques,
les os clans les tombes,
les maisons en ruines,
les toits, les vieux moutins,
la paix que sourit

Peace, peace,
peaces, I'm Moslem-Jew,
Christian-Atheist, whatever
you want, but what's the difference,
the trees, the seasons change,
the legs, the breasts, the faces,
everything becomes archaeological,
bones in tombs,
the houses in ruins,
the roofs, the old mills,
smiling peace
remains.

Zenning

Zenning into the core
of every moment,
moment by moment,
hour by year, year by decade,
seeing Amazonas
water lily pads,
huge water Buffalos
and a naked black African-Brazilian
girl, the Urubamba River,
vultures eating
fish-guts, wharves at Belén
my wife's face going from 20
to 80 in as long as it takes
to write these lines.

SUDDENLY

Brusquement toute deviant
les chevaux au vent,
les nouvelles feuilles,
notre peau,
un moment blanc,
le prochain noir,
jaune,
les theologies de antiquité (presque)
(mais vraiment pas si antique)
abandonnéss pour modeler/former
notre propre théologie de
toutes les marraines, nous dans
l'universe
fait de notre peu et os.

Suddenly everything becomes hair in the
wind, the new leaves, our skin, one moment
white, the next black, yellow, escaping the theologies of (almost) antiquity
(but not really that antique)
to form our own theology made
out of goddesses,
ourselves in the universe made out of our own skin and bones.

REFUSING

The old women refuse to be old,
the children flower in the Amazon
of everywhere, the blood of Jesus
Christ still falls from the skies
baptizing the whole world in the
belief of an immortal earthly life.

RECUSANDO

As velhas recusam serem velhas,
a criançada floresce na Amazonia
de todos lugares, o sangue de Jesus
Cristo ainda cai do céu batizando o
mundo todo na crença da vida
terrena imortal.

OVERVIEWING

So we go into the Science Museum
and see this show on the beginning
and end of the universe, "How did
it begin? Is it inside a bigger universe?"
millions/trillions of light-years away,
and no discernable limits, lying back
on this bedlike chair in the dark overheaded
by endlessness, then into chimp-orangutan-
baboon-land, Jane Goodell living for years
in monkeyworld, faces like my grandson,
grandmother, my three wives, myself,
shaving in front of the mirror, no real
violence, walls, forts, bombs, a little
screaming now and then to maintain
territorial borders ... then a TV show back
at Margaret-daughter's house, our
exploding sun, first burning the earth
to death, then shrinking into a tiny ball
so the earth freezes, then back home reading
a history of England, this endless king-queen- chief-tribe
massacre-confusion ... another
book of written-in-Brazil Portuguese poems
coming out this Fall ... e então / And then?

WALKING AROUND

Walking around in the winter city streets,
more nose than anything else, smelling
the sauerkraut and sausages, lard, lentils,
sauerkraut soup, dumplings, and I'm in
Grandma Prague again, the only sanity
I've ever had, except, ah, Tapas, artichokes,
chorizo sausage, egg-quarters, and Valencia
says *"Bienvenido de nuevo a tu España /*
Welcome back to your Spain," with an accent
on the *your*, another street down and Lucia's
Ceviche de Pescado is whitefishing through the
garlic-lime winter air, 'Why did you ever leave
me?," wanting to say "I didn't...." or an eternal
"I'm back...," night carrying me into the
warehouse district still being converted into
condominiums and restaurants, on my way to
I know not where.

ANGST

Angst the real enemy now,
embracing the grandmother of
the Bat-Mitzvahed girl/woman
last night, 85, "Give me a hug
for good luck," imagining myself
at 85, Rebecca 19, Gabrielle 22,
imagining myself at either
of their marriages, still the
same legs, same eyes, chin,
however slightly (or radically)
changed still there/here,
calming down The Anguish,
"Hush,hush ... sleep, sleep, it's
imaginary, all this hypersexuality,
mind, not body," all you really want/
need to do is to be carried further
into the miracle of remaining Here,
Now, into an (almost) infinity of
possible Thens, into (*Kadosh,
Kadosh*/Holy, Holy) sacred
(inevitable)
Death.

THEY OUGHTA

They oughta. legalize all make-you-
satori drugs, get rid of all the kill-
your-not-your-neighbor parts of all
scriptures, get a lot of tail-gating any-
ball weekends into the Middle East,
move the whole desert-populations
into Amazonas, turn women into men
and men into women so you can
hardly notice the difference, get back
on the hand-plow, hand-hoe farms,
pray to the sungods and moongods,
stargods, airgods, sleep-gods,
Zanex for everyone every night,
make everyone study violin, piccolo,
guitar and have a play-time every
night, encourage kid-concentration, walk-in-the-park-concentration, you
feel killerish, get out the basketball,
thank God for the

> SUN
> RAIN
> SNOW
> SPRING
> APPLES
> SLEEP
> TODAY
> DEATH

CONFESSIONS

"I ain't done nothing wrong,
motherfucker, black don't mean
crack, whack, snack, free to
do what? Closin'down all
the schools, look at me and
red bells ring, know what I
mean? What the fuck do I know
about Sudan or Dakar or
Made in China, suburban versus
burbs, how about legalizing
a little fun, inner city, inner shifty,
whitey, yellowy, so ya die ya
die."

WHITEMAN

Heavily barbecued beef chunks,
super baked, Parmesan cheese-
soaked potatoes,
  $25,
  $27 (Salmon),
  $30 (Steak),
long-horns over the counter
where the cook hands the food
to the waiters , one Chicano
waiter, portraits of cowboys
on the walls, beards, cowboy
hats out of the Kansas past,
gold-plated ox-heads on the
wood-pillars,
not a black face in the place.

IMMORTALITY

                         LE SANGE DE POET
OFF with another (Henry VIII)
head

        ICE-AGES   BOILING-AGES

            no ages at all

MYSTERY

As the non-sun can't go down
into the alone-snow
ignorable-ness
that papers the new-born
alone-night
over and over again,
know it will come
anyhow, the paleolithic
cave-door opens
and I sleep-sleep my way
forever
inside.

HERE

Here – Mela Lenca – Paper-Barb trees,

Here – Hydrangeas,

Here – Fig trees,

Here – Cedars and Camphors, Holly, Apricots,

L'Histoire human/les nuages qui disparait
dans le moment vert qui chuchote/ Human
history, the clouds that disappear in the whispering
green
moment.

GETTING USED TO

1.

Getting used to the Cuban-facist waiter in our hotel
eat shop, the Colombians at the table next to me who
identify me as ("*Debe ser Colombiano .... o Argentino.*") Colombian or
Agentinian (for the 500th time in
the last twenty years), the *charmante old* Haitian woman
who takes care of our room, Ça va *bien, chaque
jour meilleur*/Everything OK, every day better,
The Gimme-Some Moneyers, the seventh
floor back-of -the- hotel we're in overlooking a concete courtyard perfect
for suicide.

2.

Getting used to Teavan tea stores and Papyrus paper
stores, Swarovski jewellers, Aldo Shoes, Yankee
Candy Company ... Sax ... like it was still soaring....
or did it ever soar, getting used to being from Chicago,
the 1930s Czech grandma Cicero and brogue Christian Brothers of
Ireland, and the nuns, all believing that
paradise was just around the next *mein kampf* unemployment corridor,
God with outstretched arms waiting to
welcome you to an eternity that seems to have vanished
along with (priesthood =sainthood) everything else.

TRIBOS

As tribos irlandesas, inglesas, alemães,
brasileiras, paulistas, caterinenses,
Illinois contra Indiana, 0 sul contra 0
norte, os judeus hassidicos contra os
judeos liberais, no final

    todas as tribos
    na tumba
    fraternais,
    universais.

TRIBES

The Irish tribes, English, German, Brazilian,
from São Paulo, Santa Catarina, Illinois against
Indiana, the south against the north, the hassidic
Jews against the liberal Jews, finally

    all the tribes
    in their tombs,
    fraternal,
    universal.

GENE BANK

Snarling door faces wind-leaf claws, High
Inquisition chopper-upper heretic-specialists
at the lunch table, lightning blue sun
tornado skies, the night bed-walls
hungry mountain mouths.

Free Verse

Lilacs

Every time I pass a flowering-
flourishing lilac-bush she's
there with me again, Yaksamashing
and Dobshaing,* tough with the
rest of the world, but always kolachki**
sweet with the likes of her only
grandson, me, teaching me how
to pass over into self-ness, find
out who I am, no matter what my
parents say, downtown
in Chicago for after-Christmas sales,
70, 80, 90, no matter how old she
was, always energy-time for the likes
of me, "You want to be a writer, so
be what you want," in spite of the
overseeing of my frustrated-ex-violinist
M.D. father and frustrated actress
mother, always trying to push me
into medicine, Spring comes
and the apple trees and lilacs bloom,
perennials always perennial inside
me, although I was supposed to be
Irish Catholic always passovering
me into wine and matzahs as I
moved toward where I should
be/have (Shalom) been.

Czech (my spelling) – How are you doing? Fine.
** Kolachki – Czech pastry.

Memory Pool

In Arby's, new beef gyro, an ancient lady comes in,
Bam! Grandma Mary, Cicero 50 years ago, how did I ever
let go when she moved to the desert outside Tucson,
Latke and Matzah grandma, five years without seeing her
before she died, a blond guy with glasses comes in, I think
Kevin Buckley, best buddy in college, a blonde walks by
outside, Louise Altis, Madame Metzger's singing class, her
The Queen of the Night, me Sarastro (Mozart's *Magic Flute*)... nothing
itself any more but just pool balls bouncing off the
edge of a table called Unforgettable, maybe it's the leaves
coming down, the sun in the south, losing 3 minutes of
light a day, other curtains coming up, other lights.

Messages

Margaret leaves a message we listen to after
Schul, "Since we got back to Boston, I can't tell you
how much we miss you guys," goes on about my
grandkids Alex and Rebecca starting school, part of me
still 10, 15, 20, no old man here, never got used to
pere, grand pere /father, grandfather, still about to make
my Bar Mitzvah, choose a career, a college, a why and
wherefore, no gallery of future Foxes to be born hundreds
of years down the genealogical line, not used to my gravestone, Hugh Fox,
1932-2???

Le Meilleur Moment / The Best Moment

End of the day, moving toward the end of the
endless goldenrod, dried corn, going-to-sleep
trees, year-end rain trickles moving toward
the edge of snow, holding hands, maple sugar
candy and Chinese noodles, moving toward
the Rosh Hashana Days of Repentance...
for exactly
what?

Re-Form

Wanting to reverse time tonight, play
the film backwards, back to L.A. and the beach
at Venice, bring back the dead, Joe Schwartz
and Alexandra Garrett, back to the synagogue
Schwartz took me to in L.A., all orientalish and intermarried,
or Alexandra Garrett the day I went to see her at
Beyond Baroque and she was in the toilet, came out
just as I was leaving, "Hey, you're not going to get
away without a hug…," or run the time-clock back further
into Grandma Kolochkis and latke time, Louise Altiss
as Queen of the Night in Mozart's *THE MAGIC FLUTE*,
me as the High Priest, Sarastro … too rich, it would have been
easier to leave if it had all been old, cold and miserable
instead of being drenched in the arts and multiple cultures
where the only oddity was English without an
accent.

Waiting

Koans,
mantras,
yantras,
becoming the Buddha
as the last leaves
come down, my head
full of Brooklyn Heights
and Hyde Park, Chicago,
the Boston Commons,
somewhere back around
1870, waiting for Edison
and Ford, World war I,
the Muted Twenties,
Kokoshka, Schönberg,
Berg, The Swan of Tuonella,
waiting to be
born.

Hugh Fox

Boston

1.

You see these grandmamy oldies, well, you know,
seventy, seventy-five, another twenty years in the
(doddering) saddle, and they say "SHANTIH WOMAN, everything I
touched seeded and flourished," but
the fireside mud-pie night-sits were best, a little
CN , no more, let's just sit and talk ... enough ...

2. Subway Faces

After Brazil, mom and daughter sitting across
from us, train to Braintree, listening to their
inner voices, 'We'll all be dead before we know
it, and we'll never have any money to live decently,
your father, my dad, what a bunghole ... I don't
know what I hate more, summer or winter,
they should take Paris Hilton out and shoot her,
along with you know who. . ."

3. Encore

My first night back in Boston and all night
I dream I'm back in Paris, Rue de la
 Parcheminerie, the Spring of 1913,
Saint Severin church, demolishing the old
for the new, like all the old buildings had been
bombed, when I wake up and have my Nutella

and toast breakfast, no me importa si el
idioma official de los Estados Unidos vuelve a
ser Español ... o Galoise, Basso, Pawnee / it makes
no difference to me if the official language of
the U.S. becomes Spanish or Galoise, Basso,
Pawnee.

4. As If

As if daughter Margaret (34) and the kids
(4 and 8) were on the TV instead of being
across the table from me, is it the fifth or
fiftieth century, "If I get my teaching degree
in two years and get a highschool or grammar
school job, I could still build up forty years of
retirement money. . ., " Suddenly she's 80, Alex
is 46, Rivka 52, and me 1932 – ?

5. Sparrow Park, Sunday, June 10, 2007

Sunbathers, strollers, moms and dads, a basketball
court, lots of bing, bam, boom.... MM on the grass
drinking a big bottle of water, then back down almost
naked in the sun, no Dordognet-Francophile,
Norman Invasions, one shaved-head black grandma
and her grandson on a purple plastic mini-bike,
"You go ahead, I'm not a sun-person."

Guilt

A sparrow gets into Chris' apartment, he thinks it
might be a bat, hasn't really seen it, just wings, he's
scared, calls me and asks me to deal with it, I come
down, not a bat but a sparrow on a windowsill,
start chasing it around with a blanket but can't catch
it, finally trap it in the bathroom (door closed), but it still
tries to fly away, I push it against the bathtub with my
leg just to stop it, it falls, blood coming out of its mouth,
I flush it down the toilet so that's the end of pain, start
to cry, feel bad, bad, bad, guilty, one sparrow, not 40
kids, today's fatalities in Iraq.

WAR

The Firebird begins to dance
and all there's ever been is
tights, ballet shoes, cellos,
violins, pianos, flutes, the Moldau
and the Great Gate at Kiev,
George Sand, Alfred de Musset,
Left Banks - and *un peu de*
Cabernet Sauvignon, no need
for gods, ascents, descents,
just old woodworked perfect
flowing
NOWS.

IMMORTALITY

1.

Tantos irmãoes, irmãs sobrinhas, sobrinhos,
sobrinha-netas, sobrinho-netos, a sanidade das escrituras
velhas que dizem/disseram AUMENTE e MULTIPLIQUE,
ENCHA AS COLINAS e FLORESTAS COM SUA
PROGENIA, VOCES SAO BESTAS, MATO, FLORESTAS
MESMAS, passando as noites escutando os jóvens universitarios
falar de "Quero fazer filmes, eu gosto muito de Hitchcock, Fassbinder,
Renoir, Bergman, alguem tem que capturar as caras, a locura de
nosso tempo...," o outro que fala de Frank Lloyd Wright, Gaudi, "Eu
gostaria de ir a Barcelona e copiar o passado que torna a ser o
futuro...e possivelmente re-capturar o passado bem passado, tudo
perdido, como covas onde a gente pode esconder-se da loucura economicaa
do mundo fascista-terrorista actual."

So many brothers, sisters, nieces, nephews,
grand-nieces, nephews, the sanity of old scriptures
that speak/spoke INCREASE AND MULTIPLY,
FILL THE HILLS AND FORESTS WITH YOUR PROGENY,
YOU ARE BEASTS, WEEDS, FORESTS,
filling the nights listening to the young (college-aged) ones talking,
"I want to make films, I like Hitchcock, Fassbinder, Renoir,
Bergman, someone has to capture the faces, the craziness of
our time..," or the other talking about Frank Lloyd Wright,
Gaudi, "I'd like to go to Barcelona to copy the past that
re-becomes the future ... and possibly capture the past really
past, everything lost, like caves where people can hide from
the economic and fascist-terrorist world around us."

2.

0 que aconteccu com a minha insonia, doce de laranja,
goiaba, doce de figo (de Campo Alegre, "Producto
Artesanal"), iogurte, cafe, pão primitivo, multi-grao,
grammes, les colines, les colines, les colines (comme a Provence),
cheias de palmeiras, terrorism = 0, o medo de nao comer
bem.

What happened to my insomnia, orange marmelade, guava,
fig marmalade (from Campo Alegre, labelled "Artesan Product"),
yogurt, coffee, primitive, multi-grained bread, granola ,
the hills, the hills, the hills (like Provence), full of palm-trees,
terrorism down to zero,
the fear of not eating well.

3.

"Sim, trabalho, sim nao trabalho, que vou fazer?," os gatos
dormindo, andando, explorando, procurando um lugar
longe de mim, um lugar mais cômodo para passar o tempo,
envolvidos em seus pro'prios Nadas/Tudos.

"Yes, I work, yes, I don't work, what can I do?," the cats
sleeping, walking around, exploring, looking for a place
far away from me, a more comfortable place to pass the time,
involved in their own Nothings/ Everythings.

4.

Andando na Rua Rodovia Amaro Antônio Vieira com Bernadete,
so para andar (porque não somos com os gatos nunca ficam
entediados), uma mãe (50?), um pai (igual), dois filhos, um deles
com esposa (30's), em nossa estrada, em frente de um
Centro de Saude (bem abandonado), eu pergunto "Estou
procurando um Centro de Saude Mental porque minha
esposa acredita que ela é uma gata," a mãe olhando
para Bernadete, responde, "E realmente uma gata," todo
mundo sorri e Bernadete apos explica "Em Portugues
d'aqui uma gata é uma mulher bem sexy," e
ela realmente (58) é.

Walking down the highway-street Amoro Antonio Viera with
Bernadete, because we need to take a walk (because we
aren't like the cats who never get bored), a mother (50?),
a father (the same), two sons, one of them with a wife in
her thirties, on our street, in front of a very abandoned
Health Center, I ask "I'm looking for a Mental Health
Center because my wife thinks she's a cat," and the mother,
looking at Bernadete, answers, "She really is a cat," everyone
laughs and Bernadete afterwards explains that "In Street
Portuguese a cat is a sexy woman," and she really (58)
is.

5.

Les collines, les collines, les collines, suis-je un ange
ou un ame sem ailes que flotte toute l'eternité,
une nuage avec ventre avant de pleuvoir,
apres de quoi le ciele rest clair sans moi.

The hills, the hills, the hills, am I an angel
or a soul without wings that floats all eternity,
a cloud with a belly before raining, afterwards
the heavens all clear without me.

6.

Get ready for white cabbage-slaw, aipim
(like sweet potatoes without the sweetness)
couve/ collard greens, surrounded with hibiscus,
my wife's sisters, Lourdes (Our Lady of Lourdes),
Nazaré (as in Jesus of Nazareth), Bettinha (as
in Elizabeth, but their first name Maria as in the
Virgin Mary), like my wife, Maria Bernadete (as
in Bernadette de Lourdes).

7.

Wrapping my wife's family around my naked
only-child shoulders, in the late afternoon setting
sunlight beginning winter here as Michigan begins
summer, beginning summer for me too
HERE.

8.

Another million, another house here, another house
in Provence, the Hudson River Valley, Loire Valley,
valley-mountain, sun for breakfast, moon for dessert,
another million that buys Rest in
Zeroness.

9.

As escadas que sobem da praia acima,
dentro das colinas florestais, a casas invisiveis,
vidas desconhecidas, mulher, homen, crianças já
idos, mas a sensualidade, canções goiaba, pão
tostado, tainha, camaroes,
extase nao.

The stairs that go up from the beach,
inside the forested hills, the invisible houses,
unknown lives, man, woman, children now
gone, but the sensuality, songs, guava, toasted
bread, tainho fish, shrimps,
no ecstasy.

10.

A gata vai a Bernadette deitada no sofa, ela
lhe rejeita, "Não, não!," vem a filha comigo
deitada para a eternidade nas minhas mãos
que a massageia hipnotizantemente.

The cat goes to Bernadette stretched out on the
sofa, she rejects it, "No, no!," the cat's daughter
with me, stretched out for eternity in my hands
that massage her hypnotically.

11.

0 Dia das Mãee e as crianças começam a chegar,
o neto/as netas brincam com o piano, brincam
com os gatos, a historia começa de novo,
Hansel et Gretal (em Portugues) na televisão,
2 gerações de infinidade, estamos no seculo
+ ou - quanto? Existía a terra cheia de microbios
que andavam bem e falaram pelo menos quando jovem.

Mother's Day and the kids begin to arrive,
the grandson /granddaughters play with the piano,
play with the cats, history begins all over again,
Hansel and Gretal (in Portuguese) on the TV,
two times generations of infinity, are we in
the plus or minus how-much century? Once upon
a time existed an earth full of microbios that walked well
and spoke, at least when they were young.

12.

So' um ano cantando o canto da bougnvillea roxa escura
que canta tambem, como cantan os telhados
laranja-vermelhos, as palmeoras, a criançada pequena
e grande (Nineve e Mariana são agora M.D.'s), vamos a
tocar piano e comer ova de tainha, goiabada, estudar
a graça tecnicolor das borboletas.

Only a year singing about the dark purple bouganvillaea,
that also sings, like the orange-red roof tiles sing, the
palms, the little and big kids (Nineve and Mariana now M.D.'s),
let's play piano and eat tainha eggs, guava pastry study the technicolor
grace of the butterflies.

13.

Gabriela, tres anos, cabelos pretos, cara que parece
de Meio Oriente (Líbano), "Quantos anos que voce tem?"
pergunto, "Tres,' "Trezentos?," "Não ... so tres!," "e tem
asas escondidas embaixo da roupa?," "Não," "Mas, pode
voar?," "So' no aviaõ ... eu gosto de avioes...," "Voce gostaria de
ir comigo onde vivo, no polo norte?," "Não. Muito frio. E tenho
medo dos ursos ... e gosta do tropico...,"
e ela me da pinhão para comer.

Gabriela, three years old, black hair, a face that looks like it's
from the Middle East (Lebanon), "How old are you?," I ask,
"Three," "Three hundred?," "No, only three!," "And do you
have wings hidden under your clothes?," "No," "But can you
fly?," "Only in a plane ... I love planes..," "Would you like to go
with me where I live, at the north pole?," "No, too cold. And I'm
afraid of bears ... I like the tropics...,"
and she gives me some pine seeds to eat.*

(*I should explain here that Brazilians eat pine-seeds, most of the time
cooked.)

14.

0 Dia das Maes, um montão de crianças, sobrinos, netos
por todos os lados, comemos a sobremesa, tapioca,
maracuja, sorvete de baunilha com chocolate bem
chocolatado, durmo na cadeira no jardim e quando
me levanto não sei onde estou, entro na casa cheia de pinturas
de meu cunhado ex-medico, agora pintor, tudo nudismo,
estou morto ou em outro planeta, em uma outra existencia,
a lagoa fora de janela falando "Vern, vem, vem...,
estamos esperando-te faz tempo, tempo, tempo."

Mother's Day, a mountain of kids, nephews, grandkids
everywhere, we begin dessert, tapioca, passion fruit,
vanilla ice-cream with super-chocolate chocolate, I go
to sleep on a chair in the garden and when I get up I
don't know where I am, go into the house full of paintings
by my ex-doctor brother-in-law, now painter, all nudes,
I'm dead and on another planet, in another existence,
the lagoon outside the window talking, "Come, come, come....
we're waiting for you for a long, long, long time...."

15.

As estrelas começarn a entrar na casa para comer um pouco
de sorvete e falar com a criançada, lagoas, luas, galhinhos,
o universe de repente todo aqui, falando com o post-post-post-
tudo.

The stars begin to come into the house to eat a little
icecream and talk to the kids, lagoons, moons, branches,
the universe suddenly totally here, **talking to the post-post-post**
everything.

16.

Apos da Caida de São Paulo, rebeliao dos presos, mortos
por todos os lados, onibuses queimando, queimando as
linhas elétricas, porque comer as maças proibidas,
porque fumar os cigarros proibidos, pensar os
pensamentos proibiclos, mas ainda o pecado original
não chega aqui e, o paraiso primitivo segue vivo, a gente
correndo/andando ao lado da estrada, Shell, Cafe
Damasco, Beira Mar Beer, McDonald's, peneus, edificios
de apartmentos, pizzaria, Pietra – Veste a Mulher Elegante,
lavanderia, Banco do Brasil,
e mar, mar, mar,
sempre mar.

After The Fall of Sao Paulo, the rebellion of prisoners, dead
on all sides, buses burning, burning the electric lines, why
eat the forbidden apples, why smoke the forbidden cigars,
but still original sin doesn't get here, the primitive paradise
stays alive, everyone running and walking at the side of the highway,
Shell, the Cafe Damascus, Seaside Beer, McDonald's highrise
apartments, a pizzaria, Pietra's – Clothes for the Elegant Woman, a
laundry, the Bank of Brazil,
and sea, sea, sea,
always sea.

17.

Passam scis meses e a gente se acostuma aos morros do ceu
e os anjos, tantos cabelos nebulosos, olhos estrelados,
os benditos sempre sorridentes, paralizados corn a alegria total,
um copo de creme Irlandes, uma hora para dormir,
sonhar com
o que?

Six months pass and you get used to the heaven hills
and the angels, so much misty hair, star-eyes,
the blessed always smiling, paralyzed with total happiness,
a glass of Irish creme, an hour to sleep,
dream about what?

18.

Vem o outono, frutas, flores, árvores que lembram
outras vidas milhares de anos atrás, passarinhos celestes,
laranjas silvestres, fico sentado no banco do rio
e deixo o momento atual se tornar do tamanho
temporal/ material do universo.

Autumn comes, fruits, flowers, trees that remember
other lives thousands of years in the past, celestial birds,
wild oranges, I stay sitting on the bank of the river
and let the present moment become the temporal /material
size of the universe.

19.

"Relaxe!," digo aos passarinhos, as laranjas silvestres,
aos macacos, "sou somente mais uma lamina de grama,
uma outra folha/laranga silvestre pronto p'ra cair."

"Relax!" I tell the birds and wild oranges, the monkeys,
"I'm just another blade of grass, another leaf/wild orange
ready to fall.

20.

Eu deitado no ponto mais alto no morro,
crianças brincando/gritando
na floresta, não sei onde,
um urubu preto enorme
numa árvore do outro lado do vale
embaixo de mim, não me importa nada
quem mata quem em outros lugares,
não tem nada que ver com
aqui, aqui, aqui.

Lying down on the highest point of the hill,
kids playing/screaming in the forest,
I don't know where, a giant black vulture
in a tree on the other side of the valley
under me, it doesn't make any difference
to me who is killing who in other places,
nothing to do with with here, here, here.

21.

0 único filho , eu, se torna o unico velho,
mas, me caso com a Bernadete e de repente minha vida
é cheia de um novo mundo, Bernadete mesma,
suas irmãs Nazareth, Lourdes, Betinha, Teresinha os irmãos
Paulo, Ariostinho, Ze, todos os seus filhos/filhas, netos/netas,
Luiz, para mim o que sempre esperei ... a normalidade.

Only child me becomes the only old person,
but I marry Bernadete and suddenly my life
is full of a whole new world, Bernadete herself,
her sisters Nazaré, Lourdes, Bettinha, Teresinha,
her brothers Paulo, Ariostino, Ze, all their kids, grand-kids,
for me what I always waited for, expected .... normality.

22.

Aqui tôda a familia, esposas, filhos, carreiras que começam
e terminam, as bolas do sol e da lua, o peixe, os novos
edificios, supermercados/"shoppings," por todos os lados,
os gatos são gatos, a mae brinca com a filha, as vézes
quase luta, a gata mais velha representa a velhice, mas
nada mais, as prisões são cheias, as drogas chegam,
"gangs," uma guerra contra a ordem social, porque fazer
drogas ilegais, porque não deixar todo mundo fazer
(tomar/fumar) o que quizer....

      LEI   CONTRA-LEI
as leis da vida/morte terrestrial /celestial ... ça sufit.

Here everything family, spouses, children, careers that begin
and end, the balls of the sun and moon, fish, the new buildings,
supermarkets/ shopping malls, everywhere the cats and cats,
the mother plays with the daughter, sometimes they almost fight,
the old cat plays the part of age, but nothing else, the prisons
are full, the drugs arrive, "gangs," a war against the social order,
why make drugs illegal, why not just let everyone do (eat/drink)
whatever they want

     LAW   OUTLAW
   the laws of terrestrial-celestial life-death.....ça sufit.*

(* Ça sufit -- That's enough.)

23.

As sempre maças proibidas do Arvore Celeste no Jardim
do Paraiso murmurando "Come-me, come-me, come-me,"
mas elimina a proibição e a gente as comeriam e elas se tornariam
as maças da verdadeira imortalidade.

The forbidden apples on the Heaven-Tree in the Garden
of Paradise always whispering, "Eat me, eat me, eat me,"
but take away the prohibition and everyone would eat them
and they'd become the apples of true immortality.

SANITY

In sync with the smashed squirrel
on the road, the withered corn and gold
goldenrod/soy, the collapsing barns
and balletic deer, thick green scum on the
ponds, one last maniac cutting the grass
in front of his shack with its half acre
lawn, then friends for fifty years at the
Poulenc concert, as if I'd never
left Chicago/Urbana-Champaign, astonished
by bank robbers and car-bombers,
territorialness and tribalness, as the fog
blots out the landscape, one cicada left
and my head begins to sing *When at night
I go to sleep* .....

Credits

"Zenning," "Le Paix – Museum Mark Aurele Fortin" and
Suddenly," *Mad Hatters Review,* Issue 8, July 2007.
"Refusing/Recusando" and "Overviewing," *Drama Garden,* #4,
    July, 2007.
'Walking Around," *Presa,* #6, Fall, 2007.
"Angst," *Fuck,* Vol.10, #1, October, 2007.
""They Oughta," "Confessions," 'Whiteman," *Clockwise Cat,*
    #4,November, 2007. (E-zine).
"Immortality," "Mystery" and "Here" in *Blazevox, An Online
    journal of Voice,* Fall, 2007.
"Getting Used To," *Tears in the Fence,* # 46, Fall, 2007.
'Tribus/Tribes," and "Gene Bank," *Veil,* Vol.5, October, 2007.
"Lilacs," "Memory Pool," "Messages," "Le Meilleur Moment/The
    Best Moment," "Re-form" and "Waiting," in *Sketchbook,*
    October 31, 200, Vol.2, Issue 4. (Online journal).
"Boston," *The Hamilton Stone Review,* Fall, 2007, Issue # 13.
"Guilt," *Main Channel Voices,* December, 2007. Also *Main
    Channel Voices* Vol.4, #1, Winter, 2008.
'War," *Haz Mat Review.*
"Immortality," the poem cycle, in Lit Fix #3 1, Feb. 17,2007,
    Deep Cleveland junkmail Oracle.
"Sanity," *Waterways: Poetry in the Mainstream,* Vol.28, # 7, Jan.,
    2008.

Hugh Fox was born in Chicago in 1932. He received a M.A. degree in English from Loyola University in Chicago and his Ph.D. in American Literature from the University of Illinois (Urbana-Champaign). Professor of American Literature from 1958-1968 at Loyola University in Los Angeles. He became a Professor in the Department of American Thought and Language at Michigan State University in 1968 and remained there until he retired in 1999. He received Fulbright Professsorships at the University of Hermosillo in Mexico in 1961, the Instituto Pedagogico and Universidad Católica in Caracas from 1964 to 1966, and at the University of Santa Catarina in Brazil from 1978-1980. He studied Latin American literature at the University of Buenos Aires on an OAS grant and spent a year as an archaeologist in the Atacama Desert in Chile in 1986.

He was a founder and Board of Directors member of COSMEP, the International Organization of Independent Publishers, from 1968 until its death in 1996. Editor of *Ghost Dance: The International Quarterly of Experimental Poetry* from 1968-1995. Latin American editor of *Western World Review* & *North American Review*, during the 60's. Former contributing reviewer on *Smith/Pulpsmith*, Choice etc. currently contributing reviewer to *SPR* and *SMR*. Listed in *Who's Who: The Two Thousand Most Important Writers in the Last Millenium*, *Dictionary of Middlewestern Writers*, and *The International Who's Who*. He has 101 books published.